COMPLETING THE CIRCLE

Anne Stevenson was born in Cambridge, England, in 1933, of American parents, and grew up in New England and Michigan. She studied music, European literature and history at the University of Michigan, returning later to read English and publishing the first critical study of Elizabeth Bishop. After several transatlantic switches, she settled in Britain in 1964, and has since lived in Cambridge, Scotland, Oxford, the Welsh Borders and latterly in North Wales and Durham.

She has held many literary fellowships, and was the inaugural winner of Britain's biggest literary prize, the Northern Rock Foundation Writer's Award, in 2002. In 2007 she was awarded three major prizes in the US: the $200,000 Lannan Lifetime Achievement Award for Poetry by the Lannan Foundation of Santa Fe, a Neglected Masters Award from the Poetry Foundation of Chicago and The Aiken Taylor Award in Modern American Poetry from *The Sewanee Review* in Tennessee. In 2008, The Library of America published *Anne Stevenson: Selected Poems*, edited by Andrew Motion, in conjunction with the Neglected Masters Award. This series is exclusively devoted to the greatest figures in American literature.

As well as her numerous collections of poetry, Anne Stevenson has published a biography of Sylvia Plath (1989), a book of essays, *Between the Iceberg and the Ship* (1998), and two critical studies of Elizabeth Bishop's work, most recently *Five Looks at Elizabeth Bishop* (Bloodaxe Books, 2006). Her latest poetry books are *Poems 1955-2005* (2005), *Stone Milk* (2007), *Astonishment* (2012) and *Completing the Circle* (2020), all from Bloodaxe.

In 2016 she gave the Newcastle/Bloodaxe Poetry Lectures, published by Bloodaxe in 2017 as *About Poems and how poems are not about*.

ANNE STEVENSON

Completing the Circle

BLOODAXE BOOKS

ISBN: 978 1 78037 498 7

First published 2020 by
Bloodaxe Books Ltd,
Eastburn,
South Park,
Hexham,
Northumberland NE46 1BS.

www.bloodaxebooks.com
For further information about Bloodaxe titles
please visit our website and join our mailing list
or write to the above address for a catalogue

Supported using public funding by
**ARTS COUNCIL
ENGLAND**

Cover design: Neil Astley & Pamela Robertson-Pearce.

Printed in Great Britain by Bell & Bain Limited, Glasgow, Scotland, on
acid-free paper sourced from mills with FSC chain of custody certification.

Per Carla Buranello e Sandro Montesi
Lido di Venezia,
con affetto e grazie infinite

CONTENTS

III

Preface

My title for this collection was originally *Elegies and Celebrations* – unexciting but accurate, for it describes it exactly. Its range of forms and styles is, for me, even more than usually mixed. You will find here among a frequency of sonnets, lyrics, meditations and narratives, a number of light or occasional verses, which may suggest that the book has little purpose other than to please my ear and satisfy my urge to record my experience and remember my friends. The truth is more complicated.

Writing poems in my eighties during the early decades of a newly transformed, already terrifying century, I look back on my disappearing past from the viewpoint of a bewildered survivor. From the first sonnet, 'Anaesthesia', to the last one, 'At 85', these poems cannot help facing up to the realities of time passing and beloved contemporaries dying. The title poem was written over ten years ago after the too-early death of a talented writer who was a close friend of my sister-in-law. It was rewritten a year or two later when that sister-in-law herself died. As so often when one suddenly confronts the actuality of death, an (unjust) sense of its arbitrary injustice compelled me to write the poem without knowing where it came from or what it meant. It obviously owes something to Rilke, with whose *Duino Elegies* I was preoccupied at the time. But essentially, like many of these poems, it surprised me by expressing feelings I could articulate only in images, a belief I didn't know I had that death, however personally resented or resisted, in the end has to be recognised and accepted as the complement of life.

Despite its being such a gallimaufry of themes, forms and approaches, I like to think this collection is consistent in maintaining a tone that is serious without being funereal, acquiescent without indulging in confessional despair. In many ways, what we call tone is the most difficult element of poetry to establish without giving way either to imitation or forced originality. My aim – articulated in *terza rima* in 'How Poems Arrive' – is almost always to allow any poem I find myself wrestling with, to tell me finally what it means. Painful feelings need to be loosened by detachment and sometimes lightened by wit. Memories can be better understood when shorn of self-pity and given a context in a larger reality. Personal and impersonal subjects must be treated with the same attention to the way they will sound when read aloud. Getting the tone of a poem right is even more important than getting its rhythm and sounds right; or rather, a poem's tone so much depends on how its sounds and rhythms are deployed that it can take weeks to settle into a final version. The nine lines of 'Candles', for instance, went through over twenty drafts, yet I'm still not sure that all that stitching and unstitching has produced the desired combination of spiritual concern and irony.

The two long narratives placed in section III may seem an anomaly. They really belong in a book of their own, and if five or six years ago I had been able to plunder my experience for more memories of a similar kind, they would have gone into a separate collection. Instead, once these stories were written I ran into a huge barrier of self-doubt. What were they, anyway, prose or poetry? Were they fragments of actual autobiography, or were they invented spin-offs from what once may have happened? I wrote them in free verse; then I wrote them in near blank verse; then I wrote them in prose. Finally I put them away until one day I was looking for poems to send to the editors of *The Hudson Review* and chose 'Pronunciation'. Later I sent them 'Mississippi', though I guessed it might be considered racially controversial, and I didn't expect them to take it. Nor did they. Both narratives have been repeatedly revised. I now defend them as 'poetry' because neither converted happily to prose no matter how stubbornly I tried to persuade them.

Finally, I hope the shifts of mood and subject-matter that characterise these poems will be understood as part of the process of ageing. Wallace Stevens suggested in his memorable study, *The Necessary Angel*, that poetry might be defined as a 'process of the personality of the poet'. That is to say with Marianne Moore that 'poetry is after all personal', that it relates essentially to a poet's prolonged exploration of a life's experience and at its most genuine is neither a matter of competitive opportunity nor of academic dispute. It is at the same time an art that sets the poet at a remove from natural selfishness, so that the satisfaction of successfully completing even the most minor poem becomes, for a few hours, its own priceless reward. 'There! I did it! I finally got it right!' is one of the most pleasurable feelings I know. The craving for sympathetic understanding, for communication, for praise, comes later, along with the doubts. And then, with age, comes the recognition that these verbal footprints that have seemed so important and maybe cost so much emotionally to leave in the sands of what one day will be the past have fulfilled their purpose only if they have contributed in a very small way to a much more vital and impersonal human inheritance. In the end, art has to triumph over experience or all will be lost. It is up to the emerging creators of the coming generation, future artists, future poets – even in the present technological desert, under pressure of climate change and disastrous political leadership – to see that it does.

ANNE STEVENSON
27 October 2019

Saying the World

The way you say the world is what you get.
What's more, you haven't time to change or choose.
The words swim out and pin you in their net

Before you guess you're in a TV set
Lit up and sizzling with unfriendly news.
The word machine – and you depend on it –

Reels out the formulas you have to fit,
The ritual syllables you need to use
To charm the world and not be crushed by it.

This cluttered motorway, that screaming jet,
Those living skeletons whose eyes accuse –
O eyes and ears, don't let your tongue forget

The world is vaster than the alphabet,
And profligate, and meaner than the muse.
A jewel in the universe? Or shit?

Whichever way, you say the world you get,
Though what there is is always there to lose.
No crimson name redeems the poisoned rose.
The absolute's irrelevant. And yet...

(Revised, 21 April 2018)

I

Anaesthesia

They slip away who never said goodbye,
My vintage friends so long depended on
To warm deep levels of my memory.
And if I cared for them, care has to learn
How to grieve sparingly and not to cry.
Age is an exercise in unconcern,
An anaesthetic, lest the misery
Of fresh departures make the final one
Unwelcome. There's a white indemnity
That with the first frost tamps the garden down.
There's nothing we can do but let it be.
And now this *you* and now that *she* is gone,
There's less and less of me that needs to die.
Nor do those vacant spaces terrify.

Poppy Day

Red cross for mercy,
Red flower for remembrance,
The cenotaph wreathed,
The dead – dead, as before.

The great and the good, they
Gather to perform, easing the strain
Of communal conscience;
Somewhere, elsewhere, a war.

White dove of peace,
White flower for *thou shalt not*,
White flag for innocence.
Show the white feather and be shot.

*

They went over the top in the snow,
They really did, and then the snow
Stained red – red as your paper poppy.
They do it again once a year, in November,
Each ghost with a poppy for a gun,
Each somebody's son who fell out of life
For the sake of a maybe future
And a name scratched on stone.

*

If I choose to wear a white poppy,
It might be the opium poppy –
White seed of Asia, *Papaver somniferum*,
Whiteout of sleep, white banner of truce, white
Hope for the mercy of forgetting.
This habit of ceremony and bowed heads
Stands for the red badge of courage.

*

Stand in the chill of the present and close your eyes.
Unspeakable, the colours of yesterday
Fade into level grey – like language, like memory.
Oh, slippery memory, have you nothing to say
But *sorry, sorry, it was a just war?*
Or was it just a war, televised nightly? Iraq,
Afghanistan, Gaza, far away, black as Rwanda.

*

Is the overmuchness of us
Too heavy to hang on the cross?
Upright red for the killer in us,
Horizontal white for the kindness in us,
The figure of a question crucified
In the crooked shape of our bodies;
A bowed head praying...or is it sobbing?

Sandi Russell Sings

To Sandi Russell at 70

The darkness, the wetness, the wrongness
    of this English winter –
unwelcome as daybreak's midnight.
    Yesterday's downpour
  is predicting tomorrow's rain.

O friend and forever American,
    what are we doing here, cramped on this island?
How did we fumblingly find our way
    to this teapot of terrible weather?

Exiles or escapists, we have packed the sun
    into our childhoods –
sash windows carelessly opened
    to a soft breeze
scented with hopscotch and roses,

balconies of birthday parties,
    ice-cream sodas,
hot tar on the hot streets melting
    like black snow
under Fourth of July fireworks,
    the flags and the bunting,
the ticker tape parades
    of an always fabulous life.

America the Beautiful, we sang,
    pledging allegiance to the flags
on the Normandy beaches
    and the icon of Iwo Jima.

Do children still sing to their country
     under the school guns?
I remember, I remember how
every day was something to be
     celebrated, something
glorious to wish for, something to grow up for.

Even now, birthdays are a file of screen doors
     through which
a dusty road glimmers in summer sunshine.
     Rain and more rain.
Press your nose to the screen and find your song
     still singing.
The only tale worth telling is the truth
     of what happened.

(Sandi Russell, jazz singer, 1946–2017)

Defeating the Gloom Monster

Remembering Lee Harwood, 1939–2015

After your life died and your work lived on,
you moved from a rented flat in possibility
into more permanent lodgings all your own.
So many rooms, so many habitable poems, each
with a view of a movable city, days sweeping over it,
mountains behind, and a red sun setting fire
to an abstract of evening, suspended and controlled
by a palette of articulate desire.

A naked sensibility clothed lightly in learning;
just what appeared before your eyes
ought to have been enough. But then
there were all those other worlds you had to open
keyed into notes and quotations,
fantasy places you wanted to visit,
never places you wanted to live:
the sultan's palace, the blue mosque, the white room,
a sea of battleships, a sea of glass,
a cattle ranch in Argentina, the passionate grass of Kansas,
an ultra clear blue sky
over the golden hills and vales of a floating continent –
the ever possible geography of love.

They seemed so solid, the dreams, the memories
pouring in unfinished to keep you 'perky' and alert,
hand-holds and toe-holds, a chancy route up
to an always invisible summit in the clouds.

*

Cwm Nantcol. Evening. A restless wind. Boulder clouds
rolling from the West over pearl and rose strata of a calm sunset.
Wish you were here to share the pleasure of it –
the hills assembling their giant silhouettes,
black purples of outcrops and spindly thorn trees,
a scree   a skull   a cliff   an open mouth.
These radiant September nights, they sing so rarely.

Does the way light falls on this or that landscape
at sunrise or sunset, on this minute or that
finally pull the plug on the word machine
leaving silence to connect us after all?

Brighton is happening now and without you.
London   Boston   New York   are repeating themselves
            without you.

200,000–10,000 BC   Cwm Nantcol is carved by glaciers.

2613–2495 BC   Mycerinus and his queen are blessed by
                      Egyptian gods.

2005 AD   A postcard from Kew depicting Himalayan
                      rhododendrons passes from you to me,

while years are piling up like clouds behind us,
millions upon millions. Before the stars had names
the earth was spinning on its axis,
the carnivores brought down their prey and devoured it,
the vegetarians grazed on, victims oblivious,
no one was there to notice or take notes.

Just as Mr Jones' ewes graze on without you,
  clinging to the planet's surface
  a skin so thin
  holding a ball of liquid fire and water.

Dear poet   dear friend   dear optimist,
whose breadth of insight and outsight
made free with a painter's eye.
To explore   to testify   to clarify
to tell your story or part of it,
as much truth as the truth will bear,
always stopping at the border where language
smudges the lines or draws its own conclusions –
such was your appeal against the monster.

To stand near the summit of Mt Tamalpais
or any real imaginary mountain
looking down on a dazzle of clouds
and know them, those transmutations of fog –
such was the pinnacle you aimed for,
such was the paradise you claimed.
No one but you could experience such perfect joy.

                    (September 2015)

Lee Harwood's visits to Pwllymarch, our family cottage in Cwm Nantcol, North Wales, were yearly events from about 1990.

Quotations from Lee Harwood's poems:

'finally pull the plug on the word machine' from 'A poem for writers' (*Collected Poems*, Shearsman Books, p. 299).

'clinging to the planet's surface / a skin so thin / holding a ball of liquid fire / and water' ('Sea Journals' 5, *Collected Poems*, p. 240).

A Dream of Guilt

Remembering my mother

When in that dream you censure me,
I wander through a house of guilt.
It has a door – apology –
and windows – smiles. My selves have built
this huge, half-loved neglected place
out of the lintels of your face.

And still I hurt you. Still I – we –
entangle in obscure regret.
Your kind restraint, like stolen money,
weighs on me. I can't forget. I can't forget.
Hushed memories like cobwebs lace
this house too fragile to efface.

Improvisation

In memory of Bernard Roberts, pianist, 1933–2013

A house of fantasy, a house of music
grounded in time and built of trembling air,
a lofty many-sided School of Listening
where players in the rooms above can hear
the music rising from the rooms below,
but those below hear nothing from above.
So, Bach, still counterpointing the foundation,
is banned by a flight of years from hearing Mozart,
and Mozart, for all his gifts, stays locked behind
the singing pillars of his classic forms
as deaf to Beethoven's transcendent range
as Beethoven to Schubert, close yet far.
So Brahms, Schumann, Mendelsohn, Debussy
soar up among the few still listened to,
while thousands in the cobwebbed catacombs,
unheard, are spared the news that they're unheard.

Imagine the topmost floor of such a school.
His spirit could be part of his piano.
Playing it, arms crossed like Brahms,
he guides his listening hands about the keys
as gifts from the composers filter though him.
And though it's true not one of them can hear him,
you'd almost think that playing them, he was them.

A different view? Then let imagination
build for the great musicians an academy,
a timeless concert hall, the sovereign source
of pitch and harmony, to which their souls

return as to a master class, where Beethoven,
his ears restored, advises on the Waldstein,
and J.S. Bach, delighted with his Steinway,
improvises Preludes and Fugues, Book III.
And here – can't you see? – is a burly figure
listening attentively, making a few suggestions,
seating himself at last to perform a definitive
Prelude in C sharp minor –
despite Professor Tovey's fervent muttering,
or Wagner's, amazed to hear a man from Manchester
play like a god despite his English tongue.

Completing the Circle

Remembering Susan Cooper and Anita Jackson

Sea and sky –

Two panels of glass
stretched one above the other,
two panels of blue glass.

Kandinsky. Bach at the organ
tossing sunlight between voices,
some whole, some broken.

The mathematics of colour sings
brave as a rainbow
that rubs itself out against air.

But dying is the water side of waking.
Rainbow is not all.
You can strike light

out of the bruised seventh
of the Dorian scale,
or out of the imaginary curve

that completes the full circle
of a life's yearning
solely at night, beyond eyesight.

Ann Arbor Days, 1947–1950

Remembering Esther Newcomb Goody, 1933-2018

Best friends, we were girls who didn't want to be girls.
Nor, goodness knows, did we want to be boys –
odd creatures, freer than us but not so smart,
with whom, in class, we pleasantly joshed or clashed,
though when it came to dates or high school dances,
they never looked at us or took us out.
Who cared? We were inseparable musketeers
with sword and pen in Esther's garden shed,
tilting with fencing foils or ping pong bats,
writing with pigeon feathers dipped in ink,
swearing faith to friends and death to foes
in pink *Koolade* tossed back in champagne glasses.

I guess we were glad to be us, exclusive, excluded,
avoiding our bodies, disguising our rivalry,
hiding ourselves, protected by make believe before we
threw off our childhoods like clothes on Olivia Avenue
and in nothing but youth and illusion set off for Cambridge –
a diversion for me, for which you wore bridesmaid blue;
a vocation for you in the sweet slum of Shelly Row.
We were always a 'you' and a 'me' in our different Englands.
Our America faces, looking up from our U.S. passports,
now and then whispered, *though I may not feature much
in your self-conception, I'll be there in the mix of
whatever you do and wherever you choose to go.*

It's an accent and voice I recognise, and it comes from
the garden shed. I hear it intoned in a dream I have
of running under elms, over lawns and across the street
to the Newcombs' wrap-around, chocolate-coloured porch.

I knock and ask for Esther. 'No, Esther isn't here.
She's gone off to Ghana for good, you know.' 'For good?'
'For good.' It's her mother Mary I'm talking to,
but the house is empty and dusty. She won't let me in.
'Not Goody but good!' I laugh in my dream.
Then, not in unhappiness, I wake up.

This poem was written at the request of Mary and Rachel Goody for their mother's funeral in Cambridge on the 7th February 2018. The Esther Newcomb I remember best was my closest friend at The University High School, in Ann Arbor, Michigan, before her precocious brilliance got her an early admission to Oberlin College in Ohio. Later we met in Cambridge where Esther was my bridesmaid when I married a Cambridge graduate in 1955. A few years later, she married the anthropologist Jack Goody and became a distinguished anthropologist herself. Their first house in Cambridge was a condemned cottage in Shelly Row, where I remember them in their 'sweet slum' as very happy despite the lack of a proper kitchen or bathroom. Esther and I renewed our friendship in Cambridge during the 1960s, when we introduced out daughters, and later in the 1970s and 80s, before she left to live the greater part of her life in Ghana.

The Day

The day after I die will be lively with traffic. Business
will doubtless be up and doing, fuelled by creative percentages;
the young with their backpacks will be creeping snail-like to school,
closed in communication with their phones. A birth could happen
in an ambulance. A housewife might freak out and take a train to
      nowhere,
but news on *The News* with irrepressible importance will still sweep
everybody into it like tributaries in a continental river system,
irreversible, overwhelming and so virtually taken for granted
that my absence won't matter a bit and will never be noticed.

Unless, of course, enough evidence were preserved to record
the memorable day of my death as the same day all traffic ceased
in the pitiful rubble of Albert Street, to be excavated safely, much later,
by learned aboriginals, who, finding a file of my illegible markings
(together with the skeleton of a sacred cat), were to reconstruct me
as a myth of virtual immortality, along with a tourist view of a typical
street in the late years of the old technological West – a period
they could just be learning to distinguish from the time of the Roman
      wall,
built of stone (so it seemed) long before anything was built of electricity.

Choose to be a Rainbow

> Think about a particular raindrop as a sphere. The sun is
> behind you... and light from it enters the raindrop. At the
> boundary of air with water it is refracted and different wave-
> lengths that make up the sun's light are bent through different
> angles, as in Newton's prism.
>
> RICHARD DAWKINS, *Unweaving the Rainbow*
> (Penguin Books, 1999), p.46

And so to dust? Disperse in the lift of a poem.
Don't let that lean and hungry letter I
Depend on your dust to be forever *am*.
Choose to be rain, illuminate the sky,
Capture the sunlight's slant prismatic glow
And so become immortal every day –
Shattered creator of a changeless show
Ever renewing its need to die away.

Such are our peacock fantasies of heaven –
Keats's angel wing, the immortality
Of Wordsworth's fond imagining. Even
The last light of the end, drawn out or sudden,
Could be filed in raindrops, tears in which to see
Not angels but angles dancing perfectly.

For George Szirtes at seventy

II

How Poems Arrive

For Dana Gioia

You say them as your undertongue declares,
Then let them knock about your upper mind
Until the shape of what they mean appears.

Like love, they're strongest when admitted blind,
Judging by feel, feeling with sharpened sense
While yet their need to be is undefined.

Inaccurate emotion – as intense
As action sponsored by adrenaline –
Feeds on itself, and in its own defence

Fancies its role humanitarian.
But poems, butch or feminine, are vain
And draw their satisfactions from within,

Sporting with vowels or showing off a chain
Of silver *els* and *ems* to host displays
Of intimacy or blame or joy or pain.

The ways of words are tight and selfish ways,
And each one wants a slot to suit its weight.
Lines needn't scan like this with every phrase,

But something like a pulse must integrate
The noise a poem makes with its invention.
Otherwise, write prose. Or simply wait

Till it arrives and tells you its intention.

Dover Beach Reconsidered

The tide withdraws and leaves us on a strand
Streaming with losses, shards, shells, stinking places.
A sea of doubt undresses wrinkled land,
Sweetness and light lie puddled in the sand.
'Naked shingles.' Simple as the case is,
Did Matthew Arnold fail to understand?
Ebb tide keeps faith with all it has in hand,
Flood tide returns and ruthlessly erases.

The Bully Thrush

Spring opens the air and lifts out the thrush's jeer.
   Aggression must be fixed in his genes like sex,
his instinct roused to possess, to propagate, declare
until the beeches are his, their light green ranks
   unfurling in wrinkled flags, the apple blossom his,
that short-lived frivolity. Slaves of the system,
bees in striped prison uniforms, trained to ignore
   announcements of approaching holocaust,
perform, door to door, hungry acts of insemination.

'His song is flute-like,' so the bird guide says,
   'short riffs or phrases, tending to repetition.'
(Flute-like? A sergeant major barking threats and abuses,
a dictator in his prime defending his ways.) Again,
that raucous, anxious, too insistent, *Have you heard?*
   Have you heard? Listen to me, listen to me!
Brag, brag, brag, brag! Halt die Klappe, Herr Drossel.
Let's hear instead the *molto espressivo* of the blackbird,
the chaffinch's A flat major Impromptu flung to the world.

Birdsong. Mysterious. And heard without words,
   more mysterious – the Word made wings
and other things, but not for you, or you and me
the song thrush sings. Blame it all on the birds,
   the myths advise, though they can't agree
which girl was which in those fabled happenings.
Was it the nightingale, raped and stripped of her tongue?
   Or was Procne the swallow crazed by that atrocity?
I can't help setting a libretto to the thrush's song.

Every morning, fitting fresh words to his clamour,
lifting myself awake from half sleep or a dream,
I feel an old story pulling itself up from under,
    lending its meaning to codes in a mystery play
that for buried, uncountable years has been the same.
Untranslatable language with nothing to say,
give me a line for a poem. Write me a play.

    There's a plea, *don't leave me, don't leave me!*
Now fainter, *jug, jug, jug, jug, tereu...*farther away.

Winter Idyll from My Back Window

Naked and equal in their winter sleep,
poplars, ashes, maples, beeches sweep
a bruised agitated sky with skeletons.
Not a leaf. Not a leaf. Lovely generations
are shrivelling to mulch and mulchiness
under highway flyovers and underpasses.
A race of acrobatic rats is
taking place in the bone yard.

Shady rats, showy tails; is there sex or food
up there where bloated pigeons brood,
silent in wintertime, where Nazi magpies forage
between raids? Cheeky greys! You manage
too well, with greed and chutzpah, to keep
your species lively, running pell-mell to leap
four times your length, branch to scrawny branch...
No! you don't crash.

For me, you're jokers in the trees;
for my bird-watching neighbour, enemies,
though the tits don't seem to mind you
guzzling from their feeder. The jackdaws, too,
flap down in a noisy crowd, not noticing.
I don't get any sense that they're competing.
Perhaps these species never think of war,
not knowing what words are for.

Goodbye, and Cheers!

In dishevelment and disillusion
another year is giving itself up.
*Her*self – balding crazy old woman
in a crumbling palazzo, it's not hope
she cares about so much as memory.
Tattered clothes, frayed tapestries, tarnish,
grandmother November in her library
of used editions, venerable trash
soon to be pulped in the whiteout of her mind.
Stripped, she loses everything as snow
arrives in merciless sheets, ice, ice behind.
The Christmas lights went up a month ago.
Was that a funeral? Is this a birth?
Let's raise a glass to patient mother earth.

Shared

April at last, with me on my knees
digging roots out of broken soil.
Why, when a robin hops by,
freezes me with an eye
and pulls a meal from my trowel,
do I feel so honoured?

Voice Over

Fifteen words for the Bangladeshi blogger, Avijit Roy,
hacked to death by Islamist fanatics, 27-2-2015.

Crazed by Faith,
They named it Truth.
I called for proof.
They gave me death.

Candles

What are they yearning for?
Where are their bodies going,
disappearing without dying
under their rising souls?
Do you think, now we
abandon them, they will
live with us as symbols?
Does working electricity
have time for immortality?

A Compensation of Sorts

After watching John Eliot Gardner conduct Beethoven's Fifth Symphony
on BBC Television in May 2016

To die and be transformed into a name;
to be a star, like Keats, yet never know it
because in his day his brand didn't exist –
such is the unpredictable afterlife of those
who disappear into the age beneath their egos
to be scooped up into posthumous fame.
Yeats might have caught it in a couplet:
Keats was born when suffering John Keats died
and the poet of Ode to Autumn *sprang from his side.*

Or think of Beethoven opening in silence
to the knock of the Fifth Symphony.
Two hundred years later, here he is
trumpeting its message to millions
who casually switch on and watch
as if it were a multi-temporal game
to pluck out of airspace music of such
vigorous heroic aspiration. However vain,
what digital master today dares do the same?

The maestro on the podium, feature and gesture,
summons inspiration for his orchestra:
Bows, don't be afraid of the strings!
Lips, make rounder whistling-room for breath!
Wrists, keep the kettledrums hot with beatings!
Flawless, repeatable, conscientiously *a tempo* –
Beethoven, locked in his deafness,
never dreamed for the march of his scherzo
anything as wonderful as this.

If only he knew, if only he knew,
say the professors of musicology.
If only he could see it, say the cameramen.
If only he could hear it, say the hearing specialists
    and creators of cochlear implants.
If only he could hear us!
say the young women flautists and violinists.
What we need, say the astrophysicists,
is an algorithm for access to the past!

Who knows what Beethoven would have said?
Or which would have made him happier,
living with his music in his head,
or *being* it, perfectly alive now he is dead?

Of Poetry and Wine

Verses for my sons John and Charles Elvin as they top fifty

Life is too short to drink bad poetry or read bad wine.
And if by this turnabout of terms you're puzzled,
please don't think I'm off my head or sozzled.
Think of the long dependency between
insatiable poets and the cultured vine,
of Li Po drowning in the moon's embrace,
ecstasy, not anguish, in his face,
of psalmist David's purple-stainèd mouth
and Keats's draught of vintage from the south,
of Omar's jug of wine beneath the bough
(forget the loaf but hang on to the 'thou'),
of Byron lifting high his Samian bowl,
to women and wine, then paying with his soul.
Old sons, neglect to your cost this golden rule –
without a wine of the mind, most poems are plonk,
without poetry, wine just makes you drunk.

After Wittgenstein

Not what you say
but what you fail to say
burns in the mind
and never stains the day.
Can what you mean
be absolutely there,
a smokeless fuel
your nimble cells prepare?
Or are there words
that need to disappear
before they can be
absolutely clear?

Now We Are 80

For Fleur Adcock, who crossed the millennium with me and kept going

Time was when we two were the only two,
Two women poets on the Oxford list;
And you liked me, I think, and I liked you
The way two women in a harem must
When, grateful for the company, they view
Each other sideways with distrust –
Though writing as we pleased was not taboo.
We'd learned from Mrs Woolf and Sylvia Plath,
If we were mad or dead or (better) both,
We might be boosted up the greasy queue.
Even alive and sane, or playing it cool,
We could become exceptions to the rule
If we just smiled without objecting to
Hours in a bar with some contentious fool
Or fell into bed with one we hardly knew.

In flight from marriage, never out of love,
Exiles in all but language from our roots,
We were two anxious, undercover flirts,
Dupes of the drives we were suspicious of.
And yet we felt compelled, for all our faults,
By feelings almost selfless when they drove
Us with changing times, to reassess,
To pause, to redefine and repossess
Those links with human nature, women's nature,
Finally, nature's nature at our core.

Women! That gendered 'we', which years before
Linked us defiantly in isolation

Today delivers through an open door
A bold and independent generation,
Sisterly, sober, rarely underrated.
Where we were few, they're more and more and more,
With smaller appetites for being mated.
When mind-locked Oxford let its poets go,
We were so cross we felt emancipated.
Great-hearted Bloodaxe scooped us up as though
An axe could be mistaken for a plough.

And now we're eighty, happy to be seen
Grandmothering across the globe between
Visits to relatives of other species –
Glass-winged, feathered, furred – a world of green
Belief, and as our time decreases,
Hope we've said in poems what we mean.
Leafing through yours, I think my favourite one
Must be *The Soho Hospital for Women*
Where Nellie, Doris, Janet, Mrs G
(Too sick or soured to smile – and why should she?')
Reveal – for all your sharp asides on sex
And the peaceful temperament of cigarettes –
A thoughtful, tear-distilling empathy.
Once, after judging for a prize, you said,
'All that a poem needs to be is good.'
Let's add to that and say a poet should,
For first and last things, trust to poetry.
Then, for a life style, choose simplicity.

Age is an inconvenient foreign country
We never thought would inconvenience us.
Well, here we are. It's not a tragedy –
More like a journey on a draughty bus

Through scrubby wasteland bordering the sea.
Someone we know gets off at every stop.
We have to sing to keep our spirits up,
Though not at all like angels, nor like women
Wafted by Handel's choruses to Heaven,
Nor like a sixth form outing, nor like louts
When the game's lost, dissonantly drinking,
But like two steady pensioners, two poets
Listening to retreating voices, thinking.

'Never apologise, never explain.'
'Never say die.' 'You can't go home again.'
'Count your blessings!' 'Rome wasn't built in a day.'
The Scenic Route looks just a bit cliché.
Let's settle simply for the Stoic Route,
Not raging but obeying, in our way,
The stark instructions of the absolute.
As for the place we're going to, who knows?
A view behind is all we ever get.
The view in front is there, but never shows.
Is it a joke, a painting by Magritte?
Over that hill find anything you choose:
A name and fame? At least one good long night?
Family reunions? Love at second sight?
A flight through cyberspace in Blakean clothes?

More clichés, all but one, ridiculous!
How could they not be? Why should we suppose
Our eighty years forbid the frivolous?
I'm getting used to living in the future,
Learning to socialise while quite alone
By thumbing texts into a mobile phone.
Emailing's getting to be second nature.

I still keep lists of things to do (in prose),
Remember all my offspring's birthdays – sure.
No one could be more morally disposed.
Yet sometimes from a dream or pensive doze
I wake myself, half wondering, dear Fleur,
Why we aren't wickedly what once we were.

Verses from a Waiting Room

For my dentist, Chris Taylor, on his retirement

Of all the crowd that comes and goes
there's one we're waiting for who knows us
not, yet knows us best,
and he, in case you haven't guessed,
is not a chap you'll ever fool
by trying to look beautiful.
Shunning your face, he peers beneath
into the secrets of your teeth.
And when he spots the roots of sin
with hook and drill he plunges in,
replacing nature, long decayed,
with something better he has made.
It isn't what we go to church for
or trust philosophy to search for,
but when a tooth attacks your jaw
and turns it blue or rubs it raw,
or when you think in direst pain
you'll never want to eat again,
that's when you know – to make an end –
your dentist is your dearest friend.

Envoi

My gratitude's beyond belief.
Thanks, Chris, and bless you for my teeth.

An Old Poet's View from the Departure Platform

I can't like poems that purposely muddy the waters,
Confuse in order to impress,
Or slink to the page in nothing but stockings and garters
To expose themselves and confess.

I wince at poems whose lazy prosodical morals
Beget illegitimate rhymes.
Impudent incest, singulars mating with plurals
Are not minor errors, they're crimes.

I wave off turbulent poems where reason and feeling
Stand off like water and oil.
As if prose were for sense, poems for howling or squealing,
Soul-events thinking would spoil.

Professional poems in incomprehensible argot
Unsettle me more and more –
Words about words about words to pamper the ego
Of some theoretical bore.

I gaze over miles and miles of cut up prose,
Uncomfortable troubles, sad lives.
They smother in sand the fire that is one with the rose.
The seed, not the flower, survives.

III

As the Past Passes

Dead passion, like pain, is only a name,
      word never to be made flesh again,
never again desire's uncontrollable purge
      of the censoring brain,
nothing left, nothing left but language.

Like the four-leaf clover shut fifty years
      in a dusty book on a shelf.
Open the book. Such a dry clover! Smiles? Tears?
      Not for her, not for him,
only for that soft-brushing hovering phantom,
      your dead self.

The Gift Bowl

i.m. Janet Wiltshire

That there's no hand or cheek of you
      to touch now,
that no dimension of you still exists,
      is almost true,
when suddenly, unexpectedly,
      I reach you.

This blue-glazed potter's bowl, for instance,
      holds my thoughts of you
choosing the bowl, and your thoughts
      choosing it for me –
a compote of fruit more real
      than apples or plums.

Just so, your afterlife becomes
      as in your paintings, possible.
Not memory exactly, not prosy chat:
      'Those were the days,' or
'Then we did this, then we did that.'
      Like poetry

your visits are unpredictable,
      meetings of minds
free of bodies and words on a common shore
      of places and times
I'd say it was our 'destiny' to share,
      if destinies were

acceptable any more. Echoes of echoes
      whisper in my ear
when I tilt your bowl to distant pulsars
      like a radio telescope.
The place is a house with a porch in Connecticut.
      The time is the war.

And you are a rosy, enviable schoolgirl
      with a wedge of hair,
blonde and curly like the shrill trill
      of your giggle,
and that high-toned English way of saying 'rathah'
      we found so comical.

You, your sister and imp brother were our lot,
      our 'refugees'.
Safe, freewheeling, pampered, you soon forgot
      England's austerities,
and the horrors Hitler was raining night by night
      on its gutted cities.

'How splendid it is', you thought, 'to be American',
      noting the friendly
front porches, the smooth fitted lawns
      without fences,
screen doors against the flies – red Indians
      lurking under surfaces

of city parks and sidewalks. While secretly
    I thought England
must be Puck's land, the marvellous country
    I longed to live in
with kings and princesses and boys named Curdie,
    and grandmothers who spun

moonlight into magic thread, slippery to the hand
    when years later,
it guided me, sleepwalking, into post-war
    shell-shocked England,
where, blind to my blindness, I wrapped myself
    in your story.

So the days ran by, leaving footprints
    on the calendars –
birthdays, wedding days, Christmases
    full-stopping each year's
experiment in adulthood with pagan rites
    in a Cambridge rectory

where your mother became mine when
    I married your brother,
where the lines of our lives crossed again
    when you slipped
the name of my mother over your daughter.
    When mine was born,

we were mothers together, reading *Persuasion*
    between baby-sick teas,
planning novels of lives like ours, never written,
    weeding peas
in the garden of Woodcock Hill in the interim
    nineteen-fifties.

And suddenly here you are, fleshed in clay
    still warm from the kiln,
a gift from the war, a mystery, a memory
    asking to be opened
like Alice's door, a blue-glazed breakable key
    to that vanished garden.

The lines
    'kings and princesses and boys named Curdie,
    and grandmothers who spun
    moonlight into magic thread, slippery to the hand'
refer to characters and events in George MacDonald's tale for
children, *The Princess and the Goblin*, my favourite book as a child
in the 1940s.

Pronunciation (1954-55)

In the staff room, where the lady staff
swilled tea over juicy tabloids
(Captain Townsend and poor dear Princess Margaret)
I pinched myself to claim myself –
a synaptic spark of pain to link the me
who lived a life ago in Michigan
with the strange adult I somehow had to be,
pretending to teach
English, history, hockey, French,
deportment and geography
to a gaggle of giggling, homesick
offspring of the Empire,
who knew that *Mousehole*
should never be pronounced *mouse hole*,
but could not resist
inserting an *itch* in *Mitchigan*.

I'd fled to England in pursuit of an ideal
long booked in my imagination,
now made real
in the Victorian gothic brick
of a sprawling Dothegirls Hall
in rural Kent.
Here was a village, a village green,
cricket, and a 'villa' of penitential cells
for younger mistresses, where,
like D'Artagnan and his famous three,
we were four inseparables:
Gillian, Elizabeth, Josie
and the weird American, me.

Elizabeth, plump and motherly,
plumed with an elegant Oxford voice,
was the only one of us
trusted to teach English to the upper forms.
Gillian – freckled and vague – was music mistress,
presiding, when it rained, over that comedy of Eros,
ballroom dancing, occasionally varied by
eurhythmic body-writhing led by
Indian-coloured, imp-like, wiry Josie,
who, like me, was an anomaly.
She came from Newcastle, and even I
could tell that when she spoke
she pronounced her northern vowels differently.
It might have been the way she talked
that drew us chummily together,
or it might have been
because behind their backs we mocked
the draughty high-toned accents
of our spinster bosses.
Anyway, we were temporary.
She'd been hastily supplied
when the games mistress
for reasons unexplained had been dismissed.
And I, alone,
amid a greying clutch of spectacles
and a myriad rose-cheeked English maids,
was engaged to be married.

So every week, whenever I was free
on Saturday, or after church on Sunday,
that not impossible he
swooped down like young Lochinvar
from Cambridge

in a sleek convertible nineteen-thirties Riley
to take me out for lunch
in a rose-covered, half-timbered,
hostelry called The Cricketers' Arms,
followed by a virginal spin through
English history.
The wedding would take place in June
soon after they let me out of school.
(My flock of debutante-destined little girls –
gulls, the spinster-teachers called them –
would not be taking end of term exams.)

Winter was cold and cruel in rural Kent;
no blizzards or arctic winds at ten below,
but a thin, continual, clammy, drizzly element
that crept up under and around you, worse than snow.
It was the weather soldered us together,
Gillian, elegant Elizabeth, Josie and me.
After a bread, margarine and Marmite tea
and an hour of looking after prep
(nursing the children's chilblains in the library)
we convened at night, a conspiratorial coven
huddling in the February damp
by one or other of our gas-popping fires,
warming our hands on mugs of milk-sweet coffee,
gossiping, spinning dreams, laying plans
for a future of never-to-be fulfilled desires,
among which featured importantly,
my Cambridge wedding.

They'd all be there;
Gillian, in her Austin Seven, would drive them.
I knew that my impending groom,

who hadn't met them,
owned an ex-Army tent the three could share
if Elizabeth failed to find 'digs'
with Cambridge friends.
For the Wedding March, we assumed
he'd want the college organist,
but Gillian could play at the reception,
Elizabeth would read Sonnet 116,
and Josie, dearest Josie, would be bridesmaid.

Spring at last came, and May came.
Kent bloomed, and our Winter's Tale
had lost itself in a Midsummer Night's Dream
before I persuaded the self I thought I knew
to tell the handsome man I was to marry
about the bridesmaid's role we planned for Josie.
Since he was my *fiancé*
and I loved him and he, of course, loved me,
I was chagrined when suddenly he stiffened.
      'Josie? Who's Josie?'
      'You don't know her. Here, she's my best friend.'
      'I'd better meet her.'
Josie, who liked a glass of gin,
would impress him more, I thought,
in the saloon bar of the inn.
He thought we should all meet soberly for tea.
That's how it happened that my favourite three
one sultry, sunny Sunday afternoon,
joined us awkwardly in the Busy Bee Tea Room.

Squeezed into pseudo-antique chairs,
confronting sugared buns and crockery,
we each of us responded differently.

Elizabeth and my chosen spoke Oxbridge English –
polite, protective, clever, ever charming.
Gillian, looking rabbit-scared, said nothing.
While I, behind my brave front of belonging,
split into three: Michigan, Kent and Cambridge.
Which self was I being called upon to be?
Here was my love, my fate, the genuine thing.
And here was Josie saying 'Pleased to meet you',
which was somehow wrong.
And whatever was wrong
didn't get righter as the tea dragged on.
She talked football; he talked tennis.
He talked Tony Trabert; she talked Jackie Milburn.
She talked miners and her father's wages,
the awful fight she'd had to get to college.
He talked uncles in South African diamonds.
'Yes, coal and diamonds,' he said,
'have lots in common, but diamonds aren't coals,
and coals can never be diamonds.'
Oddly, where they fully and finally fell out
was over the simple word, 'coal'.
When he said 'khol' and she said 'kwal',
he looked at me expressively.
It was then it struck me.
It had to be either him or Josie.

Later, dining on steak and wine,
he made explicit what by then I knew.
'Darling, you understand, don't you?
Josie won't do.'
'I don't see why not!' was my defensive whisper.
'Well, you'll understand soon,' smiling, filling my glass,
'when you've lived in this country just a little longer.'

What happened next?
A lame excuse? A gentle snow-white lie?
I must have somehow squared things with the girls,
found some embarrassed Cambridge explanation.
But creative memory's a treacherous ally.
What I'd like to recall is that late that evening
Josie rapped on my door. I let her in.
She fell in my arms
before, half laughing, half crying,
she burst out with 'Well, I'll never do,
will I? And don't you ever think I want to!'
Then, waving half a bottle of gin,
     'Don't worry, don't fret,
     Let's drink up and forget.'
I don't know if that's really what she said.
It's certainly what I'd like to think she did.

I left the school soon after.
My family from Michigan flew in to be embraced
by his family, and, with all the tears and laughter
that testify to a proper English wedding –
ankle-length dresses, morning suits, top hats,
speeches, off-colour jokes, champagne,
sisters as bridesmaids in delphinium blue –
I forgot to express my regrets
to Elizabeth that she alone from Kent
had managed to come through.
The wedding, it seems, was a grand success.
The marriage for a while was too,
though it didn't survive.
We changed as the world changed
in the unforeseeable nineteen-sixties.
I married England in nineteen-fifty five.

The English slur the pronunciation of Mousehole, a coastal town in Cornwall, turning it into *Mousel*. But for some reason they cannot get their tongues around the soft *sh* sound in Michigan– hence, *Mitchigan*.

Tony Trabert, an American tennis player, won the Men's Single Championship at Wimbledon in 1955. Jackie Milburn was a champion footballer, hero-worshipped in the North of England at about the same time.

Mississippi (1960s)

We didn't belong, not in Cairo, Mississippi.
But a smart young Englishman and his Yankee wife
were just the right tenants for the Hungerford House,
3010 North Main Street, plumb on the line between
      Old White Cairo and New Black Cairo.

For us, a white clapboard, four-pillared mansion
was *Gone with the Wind* romantic, despite
peeling wallpaper and rot-gnawed window frames,
for along with a pillared antebellum porch came
a rocking chair full of an antebellum Tommy Sweeney,
over two hundred pounds of regal Tommy
who didn't want *no trouble with them sit-ins and such*
but was happy cuddling a two-year-old on her lap,
      singing in rhythm to the rocker's creak,

      Dinah, is there anything finah
      In the State of Carolina
      Than my darlin' li'l Dinah,
      Than my li'l Dinah Lee?

HRH (I used to tease him) had wandered south,
hired by an elderly uncle in New York
who thought his textile factory in the South might profit
from a Cambridge man's advice on time and motion.
If this was an act of kindness on the uncle's part,
      it was not repaid in kind.
Rob's brave advice was to fire his uncle and bring in
his own creative company of contemporary management
(he himself, of course, to be founder-director)

plus one suave, usefully connected Old Etonian,
plus one proletarian piano-playing cockney:
three Englishmen with accents, each in his own way
        confident, handsome, daring, not yet thirty.

So it happened that our prized and pillared home
became the offices of Enterprize Consultants, Ltd.
posh English vowels and bright ideas unlimited,
with nothing in the bank but that same bank's loan.
Rob's first investment was a second-hand Cessna,
his next was learning to fly it, followed by exercises
in social tact and Dixie-friendly advertising
to find a few more failed businesses to fly to.
One day, to my amazement, off he flew.

My job – since all American girls of my type could type –
was to stay home and type. Which suited me fine.
Mistress of a mansion and my own sweet time,
with Tommy to dandle, feed and spoil little Dinah,
I was free to write. Oh, how I wanted to write!
        But there was a rub.
I was living in a story that wasn't my story. It was Tommy's –
Tommy's and frail old Mrs Hungerford's, our landlady,
who dropped in one sunny April day at lunchtime
to find Tommy, me and little Di in her highchair
lunching off cracked Spode at her dining-room table.
What first caught her eye was probably baby prune
spooned on the long abused roses of the wallpaper.
Worse, there was Tommy at his ease on the Chippendale
picking at a hot dog off wet-ringed mahogany.
Mrs Hungerford glared as Tommy, with a grunt,
swept Di out to the kitchen, leaving me to face alone
this shocked, speechless, sweet-scented scion of the Old South.

Vague, unidentified emotions stretched between us.
'Don't you know it's not done?' she murmured finally,
'I can't believe that in England…from what I've read in novels…
      servants and children don't eat in the kitchen.'
'I guess they used to,' I said, smiling, 'when they *had* servants,'
adding as an afterthought, 'It's my husband who's English,
I'm from New England.' The fretful over-powdered chin trembled.
The liver-spotted hands tightened white on her walking stick.
'I'll speak to your husband,' she threw at me, 'about the wallpaper
      and the ruin you've made of my grandmother's table.'
          Then she was gone.

For all that, Mrs Hungerford (Tommy called her 'our pest')
carried her threat no further than a scrawl
dropped the next day through our front door letter slot.
It hadn't been easy to find white tenants
for a house on the fringe of a new black development.
Or so said our neighbours, Ray and Billie-Jean Wilmer,
anglophile inhabitants of Hungerford Drive
laid out in lawns and tidy brick bungalows
behind the mockingbirds' paradise of our overgrown yard.

Ray, our friendly lawyer and his pretty blond wife
had surprised us by being Episcopalians. We'd met them
in the white clapboard church where eight or ten Anglicans
shared Sunday space with a few Unitarians, for Cairo,
of course, was a Baptist, Congregational, Pentecostal town.
Ray and Billie came from Mississippi's Oxford where
'no one minded folks who came from Cambridge'.
It was Ray's recurrent joke, served up on Sundays
at an after-worship barbecue washed down with rum and coke
and a good deal of mother talk between Billie and me.
      For Billie was a blessing, a friend forever cherished

after one rainy morning when Tommy, minus Dinah,
came pounding up the stairs to the sanctum of my office,
nursing a bloody dishtowel, all tears and burbling lips,
> 'Miss Anne, I got cut! I was slicin' up a chicken
> an' I sliced my thumb. It's real bad, Miss Anne!'
Opening the towel like a gift, she bared her wound.
> I could see the bone.
'Who's your doctor?' as I reached for the phone.
> 'Same as yours, same as Di's.'
I dialled his number, no answer, dialled Emergencies,
got a no-use bureaucrat, dialled Billie and, bless her,
> Billie answered, 'Honeychile, don't fret,
> I'll be round in a jiff with the car.' And she was.

Within minutes she was settling Tommy, Queen of Tonga,
in the front seat, while I climbed in back with Di.
> 'What we want's the Clinic, isn't it, Tommy?
On Church Street, round the corner from the Coop?'
So Billie knew what Tommy might so easily have told me.
There was a clinic for emergencies of any kind or colour
where a brisk young doctor (white) stitched up and bandaged Tommy,
who, after an injection, grinned her appreciation
> while I borrowed $20 from Billie-Jean to pay.

The adventure made a tale to laugh at over drinks.
But there was more to learn when schools were out,
and Tommy put it to me on a day I had the car
that if I'd drive her home to shady old 'real' Cairo
she'd be pleased to introduce me to her family –
an honour not to be refused. Alerted in advance,
a boy in ironed jeans and two little girls in dresses
received me shyly with a plate of cakes, while on the porch
a husband, too proud to be presented, royally lounged,

bare-chested, lean as she was large, with
muscles of resplendent bronze so beautiful they scared me.

'Summertime, Miss Anne,' said Tommy, announcing a truth of nature,
          'we keeps the chirren down with us.
I takes them to Bible School where there's toys an' swings
an' kids to play with. All the folk I work for been agreeable.
          They keeps an eye on them, they's safe.'
Really? I drove back past the brick Baptist Church,
          studied its small, tarred playground –
a few rusty swings, some large kids kicking a ball around –
decided Tommy had better bring her family up to us
where an elm tree on the lawn all but pleaded for a swing.
I put this to Rob, who approved, then to Tommy, who grinned,
          'That'll fix our pest!
But we'll need bus fare, Miss Anne, maybe a lift some days.'
          'Sure. Easy,' I said.
'We got a dog, too, cute li'l beagle dog, kin the kids bring him?'
          'Perfect place for a dog,' I said.

          So the Sweeneys set up in our yard,
three kids and a dog, Tommy and Di, sandwiches and soda pop,
a pup-tent in back; in front, courtesy of Enterprize Consultants,
a tree it took three enterprising Englishmen an afternoon
          to turn into a swing.

For a week or two, then, all went well – till I began to sense
a restlessness, a wordless worry in Tommy. For Tommy's kids,
the chief attraction was, of course, the swing on which the boy, Jasper,
daily performed – pumping high, twisting almost upside down, hanging
from his hands until he jumped, rolled over, scrambled up laughing,
while his sisters screamed applause and Tommy came out scolding.
          I thought it must be Jasper's monkey tricks upset her,

but it wasn't.

I got her alone. 'What's eating you, Tommy?'
'Nothin,' she muttered for while, then burst out, eyes meeting,
'I'm scared, Miss Anne,
lest that nigger riff-raff 'cross the street get attracted.'

Sure enough, gazing past the swing to the strip of wall
that set our lawn off from the sun-baked street, I looked across
and saw what Tommy saw.
One or two black faces... more... five, six... ducking
quick behind a scrappy hedge... unmistakably boys,
big boys, who, when they saw me, showed themselves
by showing off, hands in pockets, lords of the sidewalk.
Tommy gathered her brood,
shooed them like chickens into the house.
With Di in my arms, I followed to the back porch
where Tommy was doling out sandwiches and warnings.
'Teen-age riff-raff. They seen my kids. Next they'll be over.
You don' wanna mix with them low-class niggers.'

Was it that afternoon or a few days later?
I remember shuffling, stifled murmuring round the house,
then a long pull on the doorbell.
Tommy, expecting the worst, gestured me back, then opened up.
A crowd. A white crowd. Eight or ten white neighbours,
Billie in the lead; then Ray, asking for me.
'Company for you, Miss Anne,' Tommy mumbled,
padding off in her slippers.
Nonplussed, I showed the company into Mrs H's parlour –
all spindly pink furniture and lace-trimmed curtains.
'Iced tea?' I offered, 'Coffee? My neighbours shook their heads.
Some stood, some edged onto chairs. Silence. More silence.
Billie broke the ice.

'Please don't take this the wrong way. We've come as friends.
We feel we have to tell you…
you and Rob, being from England and all…well…
you wouldn't know, would you, why we don't do it.
I mean,' it came out stiffly,
'why we don't let black kids play on white family properties.'
I stood, aghast.
'But why? You send your babies down to black Cairo.
Wouldn't it be better, safer, if they brought their kids up here?'
Billie smiled, shrugged, 'I can't tell you a reason.
It's the way we do, the way we've always done.
I guess that's the reason.'
The company nodded, releasing a little laughter.
Ray put in suddenly, 'I'm surprised at Tommy, really.
She's worked for most of us.
Didn't she tell you about our customs here in Cairo?'
'Oh yes,' I said, 'She did.
But I drove down and looked at Tommy's Bible School.
A bit grim, you know. So I thought, why not keep an eye on Di
while giving Tommy's kids some fun up here? What's wrong?'
A male voice muttered *Niggahs!*
Billie hissed *'Shut up'* before she said agreeably,
'Sure. We sympathise with that. But I promise you,
white kids are treated just fine at Tommy's Bible School.
It's Old Baptist Cairo down in town, but not up here.
You don't wanna attract blacks from across Main Street.
We saw 'em eyein' your swing. Again that male *sotto voce*,
'Better take it down',
as the delegation from white town, its mission over,
rose as a body, collecting itself to go.
Billie slipped me a smile, giving my hand a squeeze as she passed.
I didn't return it.
I marched straight out to Tommy,

sure she'd been listening, and put it to her,
'Are you going to stand for this? It's plain race prejudice!'
'No mam. I 'nticipated they'd come. I told you.
We brings the white chirren down to us in summer.'
I glanced at the kids hunkered down on the porch steps,
heads bowed, avoiding my eyes. Even the dog looked cowed.
'Please, Miss Anne,' Tommy pleaded, after heavy minutes.
'I don' wan' no trouble.'
So, since I had the car, I packed us in and drove them home.
The next day, Rob, baffled, not upset as I was,
pulled down the swing and dismantled the tent.

That was the end, or nearly the end of Tommy Sweeney's reign
at 3010 North Main Street. In any case, it was time for us to leave.
Enterprize Consultants Limited, sniffing out fresher fields,
had found some tempting bankrupts in Atlanta.
Before we left, Ray and Billie threw a big, back-slapping barbecue
to which our friendly neighbours came and got drunk.
Tommy served with her usual dignity, shepherding the children,
shaking all over with goodwill.

Days later, when we stood between the pillars
to say a last goodbye, Tommy wept in my arms, and I wept back.
Rob, holding Di, offered, not for the first time,
to bring her and her family to Atlanta.
'We'll hold the job open for you, Tommy. Bring your husband.
Bring your children. Or better still wait till we're back in New England.
There's a brave new world waiting for all you people up there,
if only you'd see it!'
Tommy shook her head. 'Cain't, sir, sorry, an' thanks.
From what I hear, we're best off right here in Ole Cairo,
Me and Ben, we both of us don' wan' trouble.
But I tell you this, here an' now,

Di is the las white chile I'm ever goin' to git 'ttached to.
The very las chile, Miss Anne! The leavin' pain's too awful,
            too awful bad.'

And that was the last I saw of Tommy Sweeney,
            walking slowly, heavily, tearfully down the drive
                to catch the always reliable bus.

At 85

On my birthday

I look from the tower of years I call my life
Into the pit: no time but space, no here but there,
No sense but memory, everywhere nowhere –
The doubtful story, the knotted handkerchief,
The where-are-you ever-present dead, whose names
Transport me instantly to childhood, tracking
The long way back to Christmas in a stocking.
So DNA designs the stuff of dreams,
And old is an age that doesn't need to be.
Some Proustian taste or scent or singing phrase
Defies the natural law it disobeys.
Life will be mine as long as my mind is me.
        While youth? Its wounds, anxieties and pain
        Are best remembered, not endured again.

ACKNOWLEDGEMENTS

Poems in this collection first appeared in the following news-papers and magazines: 'Anaesthesia', 'How Poems Arrive', 'Dover Beach Reconsidered', 'A Compensation of Sorts', and 'Pronunciation' in *The Hudson Review*; 'Defeating the Gloom Monster', 'At 85' [as 'At 84'], 'Choose to be a Rainbow' [as 'Rainbow'], 'Candles' and 'A Dream of Guilt' in *PN Review*; 'Winter Idyll from my Back Window' and 'Sandi Russell Sings' in *Stand*; 'An Old Poet's View from the Departure Platform' and 'The Day' in *The Times Literary Supplement*; and 'As the Past Passes' [as 'In Passing'] in *Ploughshares*.

I am grateful to Dana Gioia for choosing 'How Poems Arrive' for his edition of *The Best American Poetry 2018* and to Stephen Stuart-Smith of Enitharmon Press for permission to reprint 'The Bully Thrush', 'Idyll from my Back Window' and 'Shared' from my collection, *In the Orchard: Poems with Birds* (2016).

Thanks, too, to Neil Astley of Bloodaxe Books for permission to republish recently revised versions of 'Saying the World' from *Poems 1955–2005* and 'Completing the Circle' from *Stone Milk* (Bloodaxe Books, 2007). 'How Poems Arrive', 'Anaesthesia', 'Pronunciation', 'Shared' and 'At 85' [as 'At 84'], were among the poems translated into Italian by Carla Buranello and pub-lished in Italy under the title *Le Vie delle Parole* by Andrea Cati of Interno Poesia Editore in 2018.

'After Wittgenstein' was published in Scotland as a Happen-stance poem-card by Helena Nelson in 2016; 'Now we are 80' appeared in a birthday festschrift for Fleur Adcock in 2014, and 'Improvisation' was part of a collection by poets on musicians, *Accompanied Voices* (The Boydell Press, 2015), edited by John Greening. A version of 'Poetry and Wine' was published in The Wine Society's autumn News Letter in 2016.

Some of these poems first appeared as thank-you notes – such as the tribute to my dentist, Chris Taylor – or as Christmas cards; these have been included to lighten what might otherwise have been too sombre a collection. Special thanks, again, to Angela Leighton for sympathy and advice and to Diana Collecott, who has given 'Sandi Russell Sings' such a central place in her memorial festschrift for Sandi. Not lastly but as always, thanks to my husband, Peter Lucas, who has borne with me and with poetry through the years with wonderful patience and good humour.